ISBN 978-1-333-67566-0
PIBN 10534098

1 MONTH OF
FREE
READING

at
www.ForgottenBooks.com

By purchasing this book you are
eligible for one month membership to
ForgottenBooks.com, giving you
unlimited access to our entire
collection of over 700,000 titles via
our web site and mobile apps.

To claim your free month visit:
www.forgottenbooks.com/free534098

& other verses

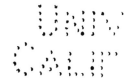

BY

ELIZABETH BRIDGES

HUMPHREY MILFORD
OXFORD UNIVERSITY PRESS
LONDON   EDINBURGH   GLASGOW   COPENHAGEN
NEW YORK   TORONTO   MELBOURNE   CAPE TOWN
BOMBAY   CALCUTTA   MADRAS   SHANGHAI   PEKING
1921

PRINTED IN ENGLAND
AT THE OXFORD UNIVERSITY PRESS
BY FREDERICK HALL

NOTE

THE last fifteen pieces in this book, which are founded on odes of Hafez, are not translations. Their aim is rather to convey if possible something of the original spirit than to give a faithful rendering of either thought or form; & I have not scrupled to omit, insert, alter or even deliberately to pervert the idea as fancy or feeling dictated. Some of the poems follow the Persian fairly closely (especially nos. 30, 31, 34, & 35); others are merely founded on or suggested by one or two couplets.

No. 4 was suggested by a Persian dialect quatrain by Baba Tahir.

The remainder are original.

E. B.

CHILSWELL,
    Sept. 1920.

TO

A. A. D.

WHEN sunlight faileth,
& day's glow is gone;
When chill mist traileth
Where warm splendour shone;

When summer's pleasure
Dieth,—dieth too
The transient treasure
That with life up-grew

& none may herit,
Where then wilt thou turn,
O vagrant spirit,
That no home didst earn;

When none replieth
Of thy friends so true,
When sweet Joy crieth
' Adieu, love, adieu!'

2

I CALLED to fading day
As o'er the hill she flew,
'Whither, glad light, away?
Take me, O take me too!'
She said, 'O wingless one,
Thou hast thy memoried sun'

I said to the droop'd rose
Awhile that was so fair,
'Why dost so swiftly lose,
Sweet grace, thy blooming air?'
She said, 'This is my doom;
Cherish thou beauty's tomb'

I cried to Joy as late
I stood, bidding farewell,
'Must this be too thy fate
Whom I have loved so well?
He said, 'My gift I leave
With her whom I bereave'

3

O YOUTH'S young cloudlet, O freshness free,
With heart so light on the winds to fly
Or glisten in spray up-scatter'd,—I
Am sad as the full surgings of the sea ;
I gave thee birth, thou shalt return to me.

Thy heart is light as the empty wind
Of barren purposeless change,—but I
Am the thought-burden'd slow-searching mind:
I am the agony to form & find ;—
The fluxing travail of eternity.

4

WEND I, wander I, past all worlds that be;
Ever have I wander'd or e'er the earth was made;
Urg'd like the álien áir o'er land & sea,
Sleepless as sunlight, joyless as its shade.

Not on your earth travel I; sáy not to mé
'Cease awhile thy wandering, Ó tir'd day!'
Say not, 'O pilgrim, rest thee; comfort thee':
Not hére is my journey's end, Indus nor Cathay.

ON A HILL

EYES that o'er the landscape fly,
Over dale & wood & stream
To the cloud-realms of the sky;

Eyes that wander still & dream,
Hopes that ever forward press
Seeking lovelier loveliness;

All the world is yours to roam
—Searching eye & swiftling thought—
Nowhere can ye make your home;

Not where peace so vainly sought
Bower'd in the valley lies,
Nor content's small villages;

Nor can pleasure's garish dress
Tempt you to a mean caress
—Thoughts that will not rest nor stay—

Ever do ye tell her nay;
Still ye wander—'Where, O say,
Lies our vision'd loveliness?'

6

AFTER MUSIC

O WHAT availeth thee thy melting mood,
      Thine ecstasy
When once again thy thralldoms o'er thee brood:

& what doth profit thee thy courage high,
      & strength so fain;
So soon agen thy coward heart shall fly?

For more & stronger strife our strength shall strain,
      Though hope's best good
Be but this hope: to strive, & strive again.

ALL things born to break
In meek sacrifice
For another's sake,

All man's striving vain,
Lavish'd as the price
Of the heart's hid pain—

Long, O spirit-bird,
Of thy lonely fear
Hast thou sung unheard

In hope's moon-lit wood,
While no creature near
Knew nor understood.

8

IF there be any power in passion's prayer—
But no : such ultimate longings have no word :
There is no eloquence in last despair.

Many have voiced their pain & answer heard ;
Though 'twere but this, that to give bodied form
To grief, call'd their own heart to combat it :
But not ev'n thus can I pray ;—thou strong storm,
All-overpowering, baffling bravest wit,
Wild spirit spurning cage of time or name,
Furious intangible fire, no duteous thought
Can deal with thee, to no calm altar-flame
Confine, nor wish acceptable,—O if aught

From such dumb need can reach aught's hearing ear,
This is it now, O hear, O hear, O hear !

9

IN love's great ocean, whose calm-shelter'd shore
Must he for ever leave, whose soul is bound
On farthest quest, life's wonders to explore—

That mightiest flood, all-whelming, torment-toss'd,
Wherein must ev'ry lover's self be lost
Ere the Belovéd's lovelier self be found—

Think not, O searcher, in that sea to find
Food for thine earth-born strength & lustful show,
Nor glorious pearl to deck thy worldly mind,

Nor isle of ease; all such doth he forego
Who, recking nought of hurt to pride or limb,
Heark'neth to love's unchallengeable call:

Yea, who would venture, no help is for him
Save whole surrender; health, strength, life & all.

10

WHEN sorrow hath outsoar'd our nature's clime,
Leaving it far remote &, like a strong
Eagle lone brooding on her peak sublime,
Graspeth in solitude her towering wrong;

& no more hankereth for petty prey
Nor bleeding victim wherewithal to still
Her hunger of desolate passion, but thus aye
Sitteth, devour'd by her own vital ill,

Motionless, nerveless, where for her no sound
Of life is, only the wind's alien
Moan that meandereth sleeplessly around
The promontory,—what saviour can then

Help helpless sorrow? What shall break that spell
Of icy death in life, that shackling Hell?

II

O GENTLE weariness,
Thine is the power that can all spirits free
From bonding trouble, thou art a goddess
To all the suffering slaves of misery.

Thy sanctuary
No suppliant vainly seeketh; wheresoe'er
Desperate grief is, then unfailingly
Is thine all-hallowing rest & refuge there.

Our sorrow hath outgrown
Solace, yet still in thine all-mothering hand
Is balm of soft oblivion, who alone
Our never-ending needs dost understand.

B

12

1919

PEACE, for whose presence did we erewhile call
With cry sincere, vowing (God knoweth, those
Prótests how passionate were) to love thee all,
Yet when thou camest, pander'd to thy foes
Weaklier than ever, now again the throes
Convulse our being; now, Peace, may'st thou see,
This lust-devoted land is not for thee.

Farewell! Small wonder is it if thou flee
Such faithlessness, yet doth thy memory still
Dwell in each place where thou hast walked with me,
In dawn's fresh mead or by noon's shady rill,
Or when cool evening wafteth, on our hill;
Allwheres that beauty's comfort-laden breath
Sootheth tired sorrow till it slumbereth.

y owei,
Beauty is the verdant Spring
In our hearts awakening.

Beauty is a summer sun
    Warming all the land,
Whose full bounty doth o'errun
    More than our demand ;
Spreadeth Beauty her kind feast
Lavishly for man & beast.

Autumn's quiet hast thou too,
    Beauty, who canst feed
Every craving, known or new
    Of the spirit's need,
Laying up a lasting store
Of ripe bliss for evermore.

O true Beauty, though joy's vain
    Seasons come & go,
Thou a refuge dost remain
    From all wintry woe,
Thou art still the perfect clime
Where no transience is nor time.

14

WHERESOEVER beauty flies,
Follow her on eager wings
Beauteous wild imaginings.

Wheresoever she may tread,
Lovely vivid flowers arise,
Springing swift as thoughts unsaid.

Living beauty, more than wise,
Fair art thou to living eyes,
Though less fair than is the dead
Myrtle-wreath that more we prize;

Relic of the one dear head
That for each it garlanded.

15

WHEN first to earth thy gentle spirit came
From some soft climate of Elysian field,
Garmented in its own ethereal flame ;

When first from heav'n's high peace it enter'd here,
No armour had it then, nor guarding shield,
Nor sword for safety, nor attacking spear,
No pang'd misgivings suffered it, nor fear,
Seeing in every face its own sweet face,
Smiling to treachery with trustful eyes,
Finding in nature its own nature's grace:
—So Adam in his vision'd Paradise
Saw but God's gifts, till taste of bitter ruth
Taught him what earth's creation is in truth:

Now, O stern angel, none can make relent
Thy steely wrath, thy sword of punishment.

16

FOR sake of these two splendours do the wise
Set store on riches, & for these alone:
For these two glories only do they prize
Power & majesty of kingly throne:

Or this: to succour friendship in distress,
To comfort humble sorrow, nor despise
To cheer the joyless heart of weariness,
To guard & aid whom fortune doth oppress
That he to life's glad kingdom be restor'd
(& thus their monument of thanks they raise
More high than pomp's vain pinnacle of praise),

Or this: to forge therefrom a trenchant sword
Whereat shall poltroon evil cower & fly,
& smite Hell's fiends of foulness that they die.

17

SHE hath not beauty, that ill-fortun'd gem
Wherewith may women dazzle men's meek eyes
Ere they enslave, un-man & slaughter them.

Nor doth she vaunt afar her heart's hid prize,
Nor with wide-lavish'd scent of hope allure
Ere men behold her, nor with rich disguise.

Nor hath she wit, that sword wherewith to smart
Delicate souls, with flashing stroke unsure
Of sharp misprise, wounding some gentle heart.

Yet not unlovely she, my silent rose,
That only may to true love's eyes unclose,
Nor yet doth stintingly her smiles impart;

But should bold evil venture, O what proud
Pitilessness hath she then, what anger loud!

WHEN thou art gone, & when are gone all those
That knew thee & that loved thy living grace,
Merged in the formless flood whence all arose,

When thou hast passed, & of thy life no trace
Remaineth, nor remembrancer to say
' Such was he, such his form, his voice, his face ',

In that new time shall rise, untouched by thee,
The eddying circles still, & pass away;
Full many a spring shall turn to winter dree,
& morn to nightfall, & life's human day
Shall change from youth's bright hope to darkling pain,
When thy young life in life's hard war is slain,

When thou art gone, & I, & our strong love
Which now Time's change doth but more changeless prove.

19

A YOUTH

Play thou on men as on a hárp's stríng:
Though of themselves they lifeless are
In them thy spirit's music shall ring.

Breathe thou in them as through a reed
Thy soul's strong message, through them declare
To the dead world thy living need.

They are to thee as the senseless words
That embody thought's full-felt commands;
Thy passive tools, obedient hands
To serve thy purpose, thy trusty swords:
They shall thy beauteous will express
Though they be graceless & purposeless.

Yea, live thou in men as their life's will,
So long as life is, & good & ill.

20

Go, book: go, vessel laden with the mind
That builded thee, go now & bear thy freight
Of man's old messaging to all mankind.

Say first:—Such oft-told things as I relate,
Such pond'rous words strung on unperish'd thought,
Such pearly praises worn by countless queens,
Such temper'd swords wherewith heroes have fought,
Such sceptres that have ruled all earth's demesnes,
Such broider'd robes, such antique jewelry
Such orbs, such thrones, such treasures (say thou then)
These the rich heritage of poesy
Are as wealth's burden is to untaught men;

Life's costly crowns that but disaster bring,
To who is not in spirit born a king.

ATTAINMENT

WHEN the strong climber his last mountain-crest
Attaineth, & the point for which he strove
Is reached, & his desire made manifest,

& seating him the topmost heights above
He gazeth on each aspect leisurely,
Considering the path by which he clomb

& which so many attempted, & how he
The first of all his race had strength to come
Unto that eminence, & how this throne

Shall men hereafter to his name recall;
Then more than ever is he strangely lone,
Seeing earth's dwellings spread out far & small;

& more unfathom'd seemeth & more high,
Eternal heaven's unchanged immensity.

22

Since neither man's proud pomp & kingly name
Endureth, nor his monumental throne,
Nor honour'd shrine, nor pinnacle of fame;

Since borne in agony to life he came
& in pain too he passeth, one by one
His joys desert him, friendless & alone,

Yea since all lov'd delights their cycles range,
All to their parent elements return,
Air to air, dust to dust,—when Thy Life's breath,

The fire of Thine inscrutable Will them burn,
Scattering, destroying,—yea since finisheth
All things, or death, or marring grief, or change;

Since this is, this must needs Thy purpose be,
Through such dark doors to win Thy works to Thee.

23

Pureness of pale moon, loneness of far skies,
Splendour of starry regions & bright sun,
Grandeur of universal vastnesses,

Sweetness of flower, staunchness of stalwart tree,
Delicacy of small verdures ev'ry one,
Loveliness of all lowly forms that be,

Gladness of ev'ry bird that gaily sings,
Ardour of eager beasts that hunt & kill,
Rapture of all life-raptur'd living things;

Yea man's one rapture too & his life's joy,
His strength, his beauty & his living will,
Each soul's will to create & to destroy,—

O thou who visitest these dwellings, why
Thus deignest thou, who art so great & high?

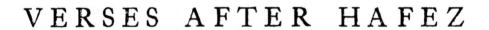

VERSES AFTER HAFEZ

24

DAWN

I SAW fair Fortune, one clear morning, touch
Like the bright-sceptred sun's first point of scorn,
With slightest finger my full-ripen'd corn.

I glimps'd her beauty : slender was she, such
As the moon's waning sickle, paled afar,
Or dawn's faint star-sheaves that scarce vision'd are.

I said, ' O my life's crowning queen, for thee
Have I long toiled without repose or rest ;
In hope of thee, my harvest heavenly,
Labour'd & waited, still thou lingerest,
Tryest me still'—She turning smil'd & said,
' Though this be, be not thou uncomforted :

Lo now already thy night-ending sun
In world-seen splendour hath his day begun '.

25

COME let us drink & deeply drown
In Heav'n's pure wine our sorrowing!
Fling ye earth's faded garlands down,
Scatter away life's flowering!

Though sorrow's myriad armies strive
To subjugate & slay us, we,
O proud cup-bearer, will contrive
To overcome their tyranny.

O earth's sad lover, drink & throw
Unto high heaven thy misery:
So shall perchance bright beauty know
Thy longing need & bend to thee.

Not in this life's sad city grow
Immortal flowers: O friends, arise!
Drink we the wine of truth & go
To deathless joys of Paradise.

26

Once more, O happy hill & peaceful plain,
Once more, O kindly meadow, laugh with glee:
Now is all earth's old nature young again.

Once more the lily may her lover see;
Once more the eager tulip lifteth up
Unto the wine-filled rose her golden cup.

O hold thou dear the flowers, that through Spring's door
Enter thy garden: ere thou may'st no more
Behold them, love them who live but for thee.

Greet them, ere they through Autumn's gate depart:
Since for thy pleasuring God made them be,
Gaze on them gladly,—on me too, sweet heart,

Who for thy sake alone live; give me one
Welcome, once smile on me, ere I be gone.

27

TELL me not, mournful Preacher, that to prize
Beauty of flower or song or mistress fair,
Is to forgo the sweets of Paradise.

Say not, ' Life's pleasance is a deathly snare:
Shun it, so would'st thou save thy soul alive;
Blind thee, & in drear temple pray & strive'.

Know thou, all gladness is God's house of grace;
All loveliness is thy Belovéd's face;
All beauteous earth is Heav'n's gay garden-ground.

To love the rose, the fair, the gladsome bird,
Life's lovely bliss, wherever it be found,
To love love's truth from whomsoever heard,

This is their faith, who see with seeing eyes,
Their worship & their endless Paradise.

28

WHAT madness 'twas, I know not, that thus enchanted me ;
What wine, nor who the bringer, nor wherefore enter'd he.

—Lament no more, O full heart, thy love so close confin'd !
O rosebud, ope thy glory, thy beauty nought shall bind !

Behold the flower-fill'd meadows ; thou too, O wistful Dear,
Take in thine hand the goblet, & lend to me thine ear !

Lo, for our wintry sorrow I hold the certain cure !
Lo, stern fate kneels before us !   Lo, rapture evermore !

—What madness 'twas I know not, that thus entrancéd me ;
What wine, nor who the bearer, nor whither vanished he.

29

SHE went.--O whither too, O one true love,
Went my sad heart, thou knowest.   Lo my prayer
Followeth thee, & faith that nought may move.

With prayer I came, & now with pleading strong
I leave thee, that my flinchless trust thou share ;
So shall God aid us, who to him belong.

Though all earth censure me, by Heaven I swear,
Though tyranny me test with trial untold,
No torments shall enwaver me, nor fear.

Though pleasure her most dazzling joys forth hold,
& luring musics to enravish me,
Thee only see I, thee hear, only thee

I follow :—thou who trav'lest love's long road
Knowest that there no rest is, nor abode.

30

I SAID, 'O heavenly Leader, O truth's day,
Guide thou this wanderer'   He said, 'In quest
Of his own pleasure did thy wand'rer stray'.

I pleaded, 'Bide with me'.   He answer'd, 'Nay,
Unmeet were thy cold couch & cheerless rest
For me, soft-nurtur'd: vain is thy request.

The royal-born, how hardly may endure
After pomp's luxury & silk array,
Thy mean provisioning, thy dwelling poor'.

Again I prayed, 'O all life's Sun, O true
Light-giver, to our darkling earth return'.
He said, 'Pray not thus: since not ev'n my few

Dare to behold me, strange 'twere not, nor new,
That a poor wand'rer's wilder'd heart should burn'

3 1

WHERE is the pious doer? & I the estray'd one, where?
Behold how far the distance, from his safe home to here!

Dark is the stony desert, trackless & vast & dim,
Where is hope's guiding lantern? Where is faith's star so
    fair?

My heart fled from the cloister, & chant of monkish hymn,
What can avail me sainthood, fasting & punctual prayer?

What is the truth shall light me to heav'n's strait thorough-
    fare?
Whither, O heart, thus hastest? Arrest thee & beware!

See what a lone adventure is thine unending quest!
Fraught with what deadly danger! Set with what unseen
    snare!

Say not, O friend, to Hafez, 'Quiet thee now & rest!'
Calm & content, what are they? Patience & peace, O
    where?

I SAID, ' Thou knowest, O all-knowing Friend,
My trouble for thee'.   He said ' Speak not so :
Thy sorrow came ; thy sorrow too shall go '.

I said, ' O light of Truth, when wilt thou spend
Thy radiance ? '   Answer heard I, ' It may be
This will not alway be denied to thee '

I said, ' O Merciful, when wilt to me
Show mercy ? '   He replied ' Till that time is
Endure thou patiently my tyrannies '.

I said again, ' All-seeing, who dost see
How long is pain, behold'st thou not then too
How short sweet joy was ? '—Answer'd he anew,

' Be not thus comfortless, but comprehend :
Ev'n as thy joys, thy sorrows too shall end.'

33

MY heart the chamber of His musing is,
Mine eye the mirror of His beauty's face,
My hand the servant of His purposes.

I, who to neither wealth nor worldly place
Incline, nor to religion's promised ease,
Bend low beneath the burden of His grace.

Since all I have is of His bounty given,
So is my poor pride but in His proud name,
His humble service is my hoped-for Heaven.

Nor shun I men's despite & trampling sneer,
Nor heed their slander, nor the infamous fame
Of their blind censure ; nay nor do I fear

Death's last defilement: though I pass in shame,
Bright worlds His immortality proclaim.

34

FAIR is the leisure of life's garden-ground:
Pleasant is friendship's voice & mirth's soft sound.

Sweet are the perfumed flowers; yea, yea, what bliss
Sootheth like hope's fresh scent of loveliness?

Lovely, O nightingale, is thy lament;
Ever to listening love thy plaint is dear;
In the fond thought of love thy life is spent.

Though in this world joy's goal is but a name,
Fair is thy fadeless hope, blest wanderer,
Beauteous its gentle fire & flickering flame.

From the pure lily heard I this clear song:
' Happy their peaceful life who work no wrong;

Sweet idle flowers, whom heav'n's sweet airs do kiss;
No conqu'ring king hath joy more fair than this'

35

Thus spake at dawn to the fresh-open'd rose *A*
The courting bird, 'Cease thy so empty vaunt: *B*
Comelier than thou full many each day unclose'. *A*

She laughed:—' In truth I care not, ne'ertheless *C*
Strange lover thou, to use such harsh address: *C*
No gallant vexeth beauty with such taunt. *B*

Or ever thou receive this ruby red, *D*
This wine, first must thy pearl'd disdainfulness *C*
In passion's suppliant sea its jewels shed.' *D*

O vain it were love's chanting voice to chide! *E*
Though may no tongue those burning thoughts expound, *F*
The ardent fire of love no heart can hide. *E*

In his all-whelming tears hath Hafez drowned *F*
Wisdom & patience, yet no peace hath found. *F*

36

THOUGH beauty's tress be strayed, 'tis beauteous still :
Though her bright glance should wander, though it err
& wound me, it shall be forgiven her ;
Yea, lov'd is the Belovéd though she kill.

Though should love's light'ning ravage & consume
Faith's harvest, & the garner of the wise,
Reproach not nor upbraid her : those bright eyes
Have right all to destroy, that all illume.

Betwixt love's roses should no sharpness be :
Though not uncruel, not unblameworthy
Wast thou, O sweet Love, blame thou only my
Blemish, let not remorse endolour thee.

Yea, censure not afflicting love : thy part
Is but forgiveness, O long-patient heart !

37

ARISE, O cup-bearer, & bring
Fresh wine for our enrapturing!
O minstrel, of our sorrow sing—
'O joy of whose delight we dreamed,
'O love that erst so easy seemed,
'What toil is in thy travelling!'

How in the lov'd one's tent can I
Have any rest or gaiety?
Ever anon the horsemen cry,
'O lingering lover, fare thee well!'
Ever I hear the jingling bell
Of waiting steed & harnessry.

O seeker who wouldst surely bring
To happy end thy wandering,
O learner who wouldst truly know,
Let not earth's loves arrest thee. Go!
Mad thee with heaven's pure wine & fling
To those clear skies thy rapturing.

38

Our toil is He, & eke our journey's end ; *A*
Our life-long ailment & our remedy, *B*
Our foeman & our ever-pitying friend ; *A*

Who is more vanquishing than victory, *B*
Fairer than beauty, more belov'd than life ; *C*
This is he who our peace is & our strife. *C*

Our strenuous earth is He & eke our Heaven, *D*
The crown of conquest & the armour riven, *D*
The strength, the struggle, yea, the failing even. *D*

Of Him all is, & unto Him also *E*
Doth all return : torment & yearning woe *E*
Surely shall pass, even as pleasures go. *E*

Yea, all have end, beggar & bountied king, *F*
Rapture & tears, resting & wandering. *F*

INDEX OF FIRST LINES

INDEX OF FIRST LINES

RETURN TO the circulation desk of any
University of California Library

or to the

NORTHERN REGIONAL LIBRARY FACILITY
Bldg. 400, Richmond Field Station
University of California
Richmond, CA 94804-4698

ALL BOOKS MAY BE RECALLED AFTER 7 DAYS

- 2-month loans may be renewed by calling
  (510) 642-6753
- 1-year loans may be recharged by bringing
  books to NRLF
- Renewals and recharges may be made
  4 days prior to due date